THE DRAGON
IN THE ROOM

IS LOVE TOO MUCH TO ASK FOR?

J. K. E. ROSE

iUniverse LLC
Bloomington

iUniverse books may be ordered through booksellers or by contacting:

iUniverse LLC
1663 Liberty Drive
Bloomington, IN 47403
www.iuniverse.com
1-800-Authors (1-800-288-4677)

ISBN: 978-1-4917-1317-4 (sc)
ISBN: 978-1-4917-1318-1 (e)

Library of Congress Control Number: 2013919556

Printed in the United States of America.

iUniverse rev. date: 03/31/2014

INTRODUCTION

Hundreds of years ago I had a mother born in Ireland. I think the Vikings must have raided her village because I have an affinity for the Norse - I am tall, I am blonde, I am stoic - stereotypically and perhaps completely inaccurately Norse.

Anyway, as I gathered my poems, I realised they were really a broken saga...strength challenged, strength lost, strength found - How to make sense of them? The Viking futhark, both alphabet and symbol language, would be the guideposts to follow on the road to me, wherever that is. I have kind of thrown myself in front of you gambling that my saga is much like yours and my words will make sense to you. This book is maybe more terrible warning than good example but I have learned important things - don't hesitate to love ; don't hesitate to leave ; and don't pretend there are no dragons.

If life is a journey so is love - it can be either a forced march between prisons or an epic quest. I am finished with forced marches. Now I am on an epic quest chasing dragons - within and without - because I know with all my heart that love is not too much to ask for.

Need

DRAGONS

holding onto time
crossing that fine line
walking all alone
knowing past all doubt...

nobody has a body like yours
nobody has a body like yours
hold me close in sleep
reaching me so deep

we're holding on to time –
wrap your arms through mine
knowing past all doubt...
...you're mine.

DRAGONS

You mock me -
think me little.

But I am a mountain.
Filled with hidden spaces
dark and deep.
When you fall unbidden in crevasse,
you will hear the beat of my thunderous heart
yet not recognize it,
think it just an echo of your paltry pulse.

But I am a mountain.
You cannot make me small.
No matter how you try.

Like surging seas seem shallow, sunsparkled,
then drag you out and down to dark and deep...

I am a mountain.
You cannot conquer, belittle or blind.

I will drag you down
To dark and deep.

Because I am not you
And you are not mine.

DRAGONS

You don't know me or want me
    or feel me or hold me,
You talk through a wall of pretend.
    I look over a sea
        bluegreen sun, feral ice
and sigh and still sing of you --

If you don't know me
    don't want me
        won't hold me
Why? Why do you keep me here?
There's life out there
        trouble and daring
            if we take the step,
one leap of faith or call it despair.

I want to be loved
    be held, be admired
be wished for and watched over
    and yet –
You wander and mutter and think about sports
while I stand alone at the stove
        and sink -

DRAGONS

In the depths of my love I dwell all alone.
I call to you, desperate, you talk on the phone.
I wish for your touch, I crave to be held.
You don't listen, a deaf man, I wave from my hell.

You talk to the world, but hear nothing I say.
You play to the audience but give nothing away.
I stay in my purgatory called woman and wife,
I watch you play on your stage
while you wile away my life.

DRAGONS

I am married a thousand years
to a thousand different men.
I feel their bodies press me.
I've always let them in.
But I'm tired now and weary of
giving them their pleasure.
I'm distant, cranky, happy,
I don't want to share my leisure.

Go away my lovers, wait a while – I rest.
And dream and breathe and yes, yes, soon
I'll answer you,
all your calls and instant needs and
hold your hands and kiss your lips and whisper in your ears…
draw you close beneath the covers –
I am such a fool.
After all these thousand years
I still choose such foolish lovers.

creating vital
strength

DRAGONSBLOOD

Family

The ones who have known you
loved you
left you
kept you
held you close but let you
breathe
respected
fought
and torn your heart
shared breath and blood and food
held dreams unknowing
killed thought with kindness
halted your outgrowing
roots hold and shred
hearts swell and bled
and skin weaves all together
a web of truth and lies well told
while babies laugh and time unfolds

DRAGONSBROOD

There's a loneliness in loving
be it child or cat or man
a life in every silent minute
a death each second gone.
All my sadness and my sorrows
burn through all of your tomorrows
as we wave in distance fading
hands outstretched and fingers lacing
veins bluing and receding
our blood to blood we share
our end apart unfair.
But lonely as love is
life's lonelier lived apart
without child or cat or man
living in your heart.

DRAGONYOUNG

I don't know how you can
  doubt that I love you.
I bore you and bred you.
I held you and fed you.
You flow through my blood,
my future, your past.
My heart sorrows deep
at your doubts and I weep.
For I always have loved you.
Through lives, time and space
I always will love you,
touch power and grace.
Whenever you flinch or cry or cry out,
never, never say it's my love that you doubt.

DRAGONSBANE

I don't choose good men to marry,
I choose the crippled and the lame –
the ones I think I can fix and send home again.

I choose the ones who whine and moan
of injustices so many,
I lend all my strength to protect the selfish and the petty.

Their pain becomes my pain,
so eagerly they share.
It makes them smile to see me there
I keep them safe it seems.

Their thoughts are careless, scattered round,
some cruel, all self serving
and when I try to gather them, make sense
and tidy up, I drown.

DRAGONYOUNG

What would I save from a fire?
You – what I always try to save
when chaos of flame edges near heat of anger or core of hate.

You - my heart – - my purest part -
What do I want to last and live?

What, irreplaceable,
    feared to be forgotten,
      needed on voyage?

What must be kept from sear and ash?
You, my baby - you.

Scar

DRAGONS

Some moments in the day
I almost feel the calm
soft as skin on baby skin
creep beneath my hands
and wait.

I almost hear the silence
swift, flutter, full of
wonder.

I almost hear the call.
I almost see it all.
I almost reach for you
but never do.

The cup grows cold
noise crests up
  and you are gone and lost.
You fade and fall apart.
    I sit alone,
wrapping stiff skin
round empty cup.

DRAGONS

It's so silly, it's so dusty,
these paths we walk along
brooding and believing
it's important, right or wrong –
we wonder and we worry
Are we fat? Or are we strong?
Are we pretty? Are we smart? Are we wanted? Are we wrong?
All the fretting, all the questions,
All the pointless care
Why does it matter where we are
As long as we're all there ?

DRAGONSDEATH

I have been betrayed
by you and your so-called love.
I have held you crying in my arms
and whispered for your salve -
I have watched your years
etch dullness on my skin
have cursed and sworn and cried.
Perhaps it is our tears that
touch and turn to blood -
Maybe tears' blood drains the
heart, tears tear the vital breath -
I only know I watched you die
and simply can't imagine
the corpse that walks away from me
is you - both dead and death begotten.

DRAGONJOY

There can never be too much, too little
Too tomorrow or too past
Live, drink it in and swallow
For all is fading fast
Don't wish.
Don't want.
Don't wonder.
Do and take and hold
Give back
Call joy as given - be free, be ever bold

Nails clenched and iron driven
Clutch always onto time
Pull life close with open hands
Water drifts with sand

DRAGONSTIME

warm my belly
feed my tongue
soft my eyes
keep me young
hold me still
send me forth
circle world
hold my course
life still calls
heart still sings
blood still pounds
red magic rings
stay not still
hold not dream
curse and course
billow and stream
time recedes
bloodlet dreams

DRAGONBITTER

I have a capacity for pity
that takes my brains away.
A selfless senseless moment
which holds my heart in sway.
Even as my hate and sorrow flood my veins and eyes
I see you sad and selfness naked, a faltering disguise
I want to run and hide
and tear and burn … . yet
I heed my softer side and turn
even through my rising gorge, the choking sense of fury
I curl against your side not safe, not sure but sorry.

DRAGONTRAP

It's not too late.

Things that hold us
bind us, shred us, blind us.

Shame that stops us
blame that tightens
years of passing
marks that scar us
marks that tie us
make us lie.

Not upon the bed we wish
not with what or who or which
Nothing we have loved and lost,
nothing we have sought and sent.
We tremble, gently bleed
heart's blood, a breath, a need.
There is not enough, we meld,
we build, defy the truth
the sad, the brute.
We fear the end of what we know.
But what we know is fearful still
binds us, bleeds us, keeps us still
to lie with strangers and turn from will.

DRAGONSBANE

Fingers, flesh localized
  laser beamed,
    erotic

I dream of fingers burning flesh,
    trailing dreams
      exotic

Flesh tips connecting bridges,
    tying dreams,
      tangling nerves

I wish, I want, I breathe
    holding
      haven
        heaven

exhale
  exhaust then
    exit

Hold tight a dream wish hard
Bone braces then retreats
and waits, I want,
but it's not this.

DRAGONSBANE

To only want the flesh
skin hunger and deep breath
to suck in depth and width
to let go all else of self
what next?
I starve, I hold, I fashion
a life of shallow means.
I want an ocean.
I want safe harbor,
but not by any means.
Do you want to hold me?
I will hold you still
My breath will feed your soul
My flesh will ease your sorrow
My blood will stop your wounds
I will give you all I hold
But –
But—
Will you take it in?
Will you hold it safe?
Or will you let it dribble,
drain and slide away from
safe and saving place?

Then I will die of longing
and you will die of waste.

Ice

DRAGONSHOPE

What is in my heart?
What you have put there:
anger, rust and heavy things,
blades and broken bits of glass.
You hid in my life as I laughed;
you drank it down until I gasped,
choked and cried aloud.

You told me not to bleed,
not to stare wide-eyed with loneliness,
not to shiver with despair.
You told me let life roll off my back,
to copy ducks and tears,
for tears are only water
and fears are silly things.
You promised me life held much
worse than bits of blood
and ripped heartstrings.
And you were right.
But mostly wrong -
because there are small things that grow through broken hearts
like pansies under stone
small things that grow
and stretch and heal and
become forevermore.

DRAGONSFEAR

You don't even know my sorrows
You haven't seen my pain
You eat, you drink, you watch TV.
Where am I again?
I drift and weep
I crave more sleep
I want to be alone.
You don't see me
You don't let me be
You never even welcome me.
I yearn for home,
for place, for hold,
a keep that's mine,
a time, a time unlocked and soft,
a touch beyond that holds my dream....
I wish I might,
I wish I may,
I wish, I wish
my life away...

DRAGONSHOPE

As all the points of life
shatter, shine and dance,
I wonder at the pain,
the pointlessness, the chance.

I want to build a refuge,
a place to hold the hurt.
I want a fort, a bastion,
stand of strength and stone.
I want a place to rest,
to sleep perchance, to dream
a home where all beings gather,
slide and seem.
There is neither a before and seldom happy after,
but there is now
and then is now
and now is ever after.

Safe, shatter, shining,
gleaming, breathing,
holding, seeming,
    hold –
      breathe –
        and take grasp

Life matters
    life lasts.

DRAGONYOUNG

I am sad today:
sad with the longing for all the past
aching for hope
wanting comfort
desiring adventure.

And all there is—is me.

I must hold myself
and love the others.

Spread thin my strength
and catch them all.

I shrink from need and
hold my breath—it hurts.

And then I feel the touch—
the wind, the breeze, the past.

I do not know. I can't remember.
I fear and then I hear—

Their fragility, life stretched
invisible on change, ringing like chimes.

I see them from the corner of my eye.
For what they take they give back two-fold.
For all I hold them
they hold me too.
For all that I love them
their love breaks my heart and floods my very being.

We are a murder of crows,
clever, daring, and bad,
a band of living birds,
bright and quick and transient.
We are ourselves bound by
all our past lives and the threat of what may come,
always together, always we are
strong and safe and known by heart.

DRAGONCAUGHT

if all I want is a dream,
be had and held and looked upon,
if all I need is breath and bread and breadth of hope,
then let me stay.

let me wait and wish and want,
I promise not to pray,
I promise just to touch with eyes and keep my hands at bay.
I promise to twist my fingers tight together,
as you whisper notwords on my flesh.
I promise to wait and wish and want and watch
you love the rest.
Watch you love yourself, love your power and ego best.

Let me wait and wish and want
and starve and waste away.
"That's the price of loving me" you smile and smooth your face.
"I'm worth it all and so much more, you're lucky I let you stay."

DRAGONCAUGHT

You do me no favors.
You say it's okay, "I have seen your naked body."
You do me no favors.
I don't need your permission,
your allowance of existence,
your puerile approval of physical.
You do me no favors.

My body is a triumph –
borne children – held pain – given solace.
I am a mountain.
  I am an ocean.
    I shine in sunlight,
lie deep in the dark.
My scars are from wounds survived,
    battles fought.

You do me no favors
when you do not see me—
the glorious skeleton inside.
  Strong, free, powerful,
only held in this life by sinews of love.

I tower above you,
and all you can see is a small sliver of me because your eyes
cannot open wide.
You are not so favored.

DRAGONYOUNG

The family is a place where
small things gather 'round.

Doors open and drawers close.
You never know where secrets are stowed,
but you know they are there.

You know the small things
that drape over you, sleep and twitch
and stare with other eyes.

You know your breath beats
still and same and shared.

You know hearts shadow each
and wind winds each 'round
and sleep wraps you all in one.

You know why you breathe.
You know that blood traces through.
You know that dreams ease
over like small waves on
sand leaving one endless shared pattern.
You know this is family.

DRAGONLOVE

I want to fall laughing into bed,
  heart wide open, eyes glittering joy.
I want to fall into sleep
  down to deepest rest against warm breath.
I want my heart to wait then catch your beat
  and have our blood run slow together,
I want to trust that time
  will hold your promise true.
I want to know you sigh with me
  while our dreams tangle like sheets.

I am done with guarding my soul from onslaught, of licking wounds,
regaining strength and trying yet again.
There has been death in this bed, and I am done watching it.

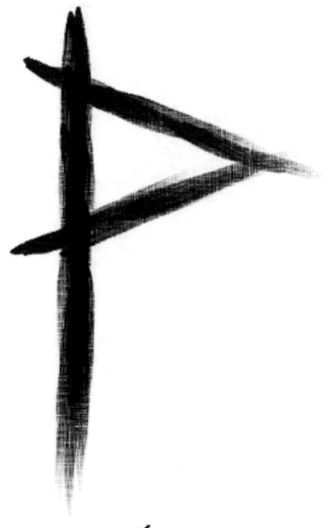

Chaos

DRAGONBITTER

You are the enemy.

Slayer of smiles
Thief of laughter
    Murderer

Faces freeze when you walk through,
hearts beat, stop, halt,
    strive.
Breath catches,
    love falters.
You trail fear like tattered feathers.

We hate you,
  your scratching fingers,
    your strangling grasp.

We make you angry—
  you don't know why we laugh
  or even why we flee.
    Murderer.

You torture love out of us.
Never enough—you may ever plead,
then choke the moment—
    we suffocate, we bleed.
No matter—we still live!
  And scurry 'round the corners

  to savour love.

We are one - you are alone.

You say you are the power,
  The One who has the say,
we are supposed to tremble,
we wish you'd go away.
we don't want to do that,
we don't want to be your prey,
we don't want you with us,

You are love gone far astray.

DRAGONBITTER

When your flesh melts into mine,
are we married? Then?

When our eyes are lost and locked, heart melted,
are we married? Then?

When our child melts into me for refuge safe from you,
are we married? Now?

When our flesh melts away, dead and softly gone,
are we still married?

DRAGONBITTER

When I wish for more,
        who comes?
When I sigh, sleepless,
        who draws my dreams?
When I do dream and see through dark,
        who holds my breath?
Who calls my lips?

Not you, not now.
A promise broken,
not here, not deeply.
Your love unspoken
dried deep in blood,
held still in breath.
I sorrow more,
I love you less.

DRAGONBITTER

"Mother and Wife"

And when in the deep of days,
spent watching life and all your ways,
do I wish, or hope, or prevaricate,
do I tell a tale, a lie too late?

Do I make it happen,
keep centre still,
hold quake from earth
and gale from hill?

Do I hold all threads of love and life,
weave in and out to bury strife,
blind my heart, still be your wife?

Do I do all this for love of you?

Do I close my eyes to see your face as whisper claws, "Love, hold a space."
Or do I know, in my being,
that time and blood beyond your seeing
are threads of hope and coming dread?
My weaving pulls them through our ways,
the lies and love and death of days.

DRAGONYOUNG

Sometimes the love, fierce, unburdened,
comes raging forth uncalled, unsought, not stopped and undenied.

Bearclaw strong it wipes clean time—no prints, no touch, nothing
stands.

Delicate, surgical, unbending, clawdeep - it cuts my heart. I bleed.
I weep.

I love you child, you're mine to keep
just now, not ever, a wish, a sleep.

You rise and walk and catch your dreams
I stay, I wish, I age—I silent-scream
"My love is strong, clawdeep, clawlong."
I give you love and then you're gone....

DRAGONBITTER

I have learned to love loneliness,
    married to you.
I have learned to need solitude,
    married to you.

I have desire for safe place,
    constant flesh,
yet known it to mean nothing,
    give nothing, give less.

I have leaned on my children,
felt their pain, bled their loss.
I have gathered them to me,
I have held them aloft.

I have hoped, I have dreamed,
waited, wanted and seemed.
But nothing, still nothing,
there's nothing, it seems.

We laugh behind hands, lower eyes
and share shadows, invisible people like stones on the ground,
stones that hide us,
protect us, divide us… from you.

We feel happy and safe
unseen, unassaulted and strong
while you strut around us
thinking nothing is wrong.

We dance—you won't see us.
You talk—we won't hear.
We've learned to love solitude
whenever you're near.

DRAGONLOVE

I wish that you could love me
as I have loved you past:
deep and calm and clear,
accepting and expanding,
excusing and explaining,
scrambling and complaining.

I have rewritten your biggest part
and tweaked with bits omitted;
the public realm will never see
the pain you have delivered.

I only ask, no, beg you; ease,
wait, hold back, not burden
with dreadful touch, the final blow,
a death by carelessness.
Neglect and soft abuse your jagged humor,
the silence of no laughter.
It is possible to talk someone to death.

DRAGONMAGIC

I pull the magic through my fingers
feel the earth that comes between us
know the pulse, the breathing death
nothing more and nothing less.

All the colours spin around us
all the shapes smell fresh and clear
all the hopes shatter bells
all the vultures shudder near.

At the point of life and dying
on the blade of youth and age
at the sound of fear and laughter
what has gone before comes after.

There is a power in not knowing
pulling threads of fire not burning
lying fallow—no small creatures,
empty eyes, empty features.

There is a moment we all know
when there is no air.
No breath to catch in fear.
Flares the fire, fallowing done,
small life crawls from death to sun.

DRAGONSTRONG

I don't want to sleep with you.
I don't want to touch you.
You pull me through your fingers.
You hold me till I cry.
My breath may sob in silence;
do I wait for one to die?

I don't want the time to fade.
I don't want the edges frayed.
Don't pull the only thread
that holds the centre still.
Your fingers so carelessly
flash and flick and kill.

I fall away, outstretched,
outflanked, outraged.
I spin away from all you know
and as I fly, terrified, I hold
true and fast and strong to this -
Breathe in breathe out
You're wrong.

DRAGONBITTER

Marriage lies
like a lion waiting
teeth bared
sixty second mating

Blood stains
Earth drains
Bones bleach
Hearts leach

Female hunts
Young feed
Male calls
Male needs

DRAGONCOLD

I feel my skin thicken at your touch,
growing fast around like snake scale.

I zipper up to lowered chin,
a coat against your chill.
You've never touched my real flesh,
and now you never will.

DRAGONSFEAR

If I called for help,
would you answer me?

If I drifted in the sea,
would you dare to swim to me?

I look at all the past,
what the future threatens.

I watch the veins in my flesh thicken,
pulse and weather.

I fear age and death and loneliness.
I want my mother near.

I wish, I wish I could look at you
and not feel this fear.

DRAGONSGOLD

Words cling to me as I walk through time,
crawl up my soul
and sigh out through my lips.
They wrap around my fingers
until I shake them off,
brushing them onto paper.
Then they look up at me and
my eyes love them.
They are me, mine,
and I give them to you.

DRAGONSSIGHT

I see the broken thing
in all of us
that wants a touch
a softness.
In some it bites—
it tears the heart
of all who come too near.
In some it waits
like a lost hope
for space and warmth
and chance.

It may be or maybe,
not or never come,
but still waits,
the brokenwinged.

DRAGONSEND

things that climb
things that hang
things that pull their faces back—
bones that twist
lips that hiss
small spineless things that claw

Death sighs and smiles
a toothy grin
everything begins again
shredded bone
splintered teeth
stunted baby lies beneath

huddled Masses call the night
yet still one dark hope—
one shard so sleight
pierces vein of gold and light
Death sighs and chuckles and turns around
lost a moment in silent sound

DRAGONSLOVE

The touch of a feather,
the claw of a bear,
me gathered in—
the world out there.

The comfort of fierce,
the protection of longing,
the fragile home cover,
the aching belonging.

What more,
what less,
who wanting,
what missing?

The brown strength of bear,
the white safety of wing.
All hold, all call, all bring -
me gathered in and the world out there.

DRAGONSCURSE

white finger traces her
escape route,
cross flesh, down ribs,
through bone.

her hands touch, and
feel and need,
whenever he comes home.

white hands clench, and
pull and fall away,
useless at her side.

DRAGONYOUNG

I have my children
she holds the thought
they grow through me
reach me, shade me, keep me.
They are themselves
my need, my thirst
they were given to me first
not just, not last,
not forever—for now.

For now.
She holds the dread at bay,
she holds the wave,
she kneads the day.
The moments are threaded,
beaded, embedded,
burned deep and soft forever.
The scars and trails and whispers
are always hers.

Love

Sun
Warmness

DRAGONYOUNG

I will leave it go
   let it fly

Breathe deep while all around
   children cry

I will make them safe
   draw battle lines
   let none cross
   let none die

The margins smudge
   my colours fade

I breathe deep
   refuse afraid

When all expect, demand and hope
   I circle power
   find my brave
   and warm myself.

I cradle love
   I make it last.

DRAGONDREAM

I want to talk to the dead,
touch the ghosts of my past.
I want to feel their eyes upon me,
their stillness holding fast.
I want to close my eyes and hear
soft breathing gently sigh,
then open eyes to see
my father sliding by.
I want my past to hold me.
I want the days to slow.
I want my living to stay close.
And my dead stay closer still.

DRAGONLOVE

I need to be held,
to hear nothing, see all.
I twist in your arms,
black into night.
Never let go; hold me fast,
hold me tight.
Hearts beating, blood flowing,
soft into sleep.

I need to be held
in case I should fall.
I need to be held,
hear nothing, see all.
Keep hold of life, hear not the call,
keep breath, keep blood running,
never leave me behind.

I need to be held.
I'll hold you—you're fine.
We'll keep the balance
and cling to the edge,
twist as we will,
but fall and we're dead.

DRAGONYOUNG

I crave a comfort you can't give me,
a knowledge you don't have,
a certainty too uncertain,
it leaves me hungry, angry, sad.

I carve my name in children
and set them on a path.
I wonder where they'll lead me,
what deep despair, what past?
I finally, humble, starving,
creep to place unknown,
sit silent, unbid, unwanted,
ultimately alone.

Then in my heart I feel
the beat of some deep thought.
Reach dry scaly hand gently
to touch my child, my love.

DRAGONSBANE

I look in the mirror. I am old—
not as old as my mother but near.
I look in my heart, ache for what's gone,
what I want, what I fear.
My children grown, my love withered small,
a pale and quiet scream.
I look back on the years
I look out to sea-swallowing waves—
will they hold me or drown me?
I feel my breath, my heart seizes,
my eyes blind with tears.
What dare I hold?
My choices are less.

DRAGONSREST

All the skulls of dragons
lie empty on the beach.
Rocks carved by water-loving
reach into sand bone deep.
Stretch down and find the darkness,
slice coral into meat,
sip blood and drink green sunlight,
sink to rest replete.
Rocks cry out in terror,
wind whips them down to dust.
Deadly waves intent on ruin
slide off the stone-dead beasts.
All their power and their glory
slips beneath the foam.
All the dragon stories, all the dragons' homes,
glisten, crack and call them down,
where they sleep alone.

insight

wakefulness

DRAGONSTRONG

Prove me wrong?
Make you strong?
Give way to subtle play?

If not now, if not how,
I will my heart to stay.

It makes no sense to grow so old
so sad, so fiercely frail.

Why wait until the bones bleed out,
until my skin thins dry?

Breathe deep, breathe wide, slide
hand beneath old scars and pull life free.

Hold life in twisted fingers,
toss it to the deep wide sky.

A thousand bits of crashing dreams glitter in confusion.
I catch my breath wide and deep.

I prove you wrong.
I make me strong.

DRAGONSBANE

So we all know the random factor
the hairbreadth link of life

One touch here, one
death there and
all will be forgotten

Watch closely as each one's
breath pulls air from one and other

Focus eyes at narrow light
what grows destroys, what kills, brings life
forgotten, misbegotten

if you would see a pattern
hold tight to thread of light

follow path through pain and fear
catch in all those you love
keep them fiercely near

One touch life one touch death
nothing is forgotten.

DRAGONSTRONG

Never turn away.
Never take the coward's way.
It is not braver to stand and fight,
to hold all stone against the night.

Do not think, believe or vow
that you would defy or give your all –
To what?
To hold a lie the truth?
To feed another's need?
You cannot give yourself to others' appetite
You cannot sow and feed and fight –

Just slide away, make haste, seize day,
ease on out the door.
Blink at the sudden edge.
There is a brightness here—a rightness,
a soft step of chance and end of chase,
a choice, a trust.
Just make… and take and smile and wake…

DRAGONFREE

If all the dragons in the world
    answered to my call,
if they wound and bound themselves
    about my ankles and my doubts,
I would still somebit fear you.

You scratch, you drag lazy claw,
    threaten sinew and tear soul.
You make me still my heart,
    freeze thought and joy away
and cower, even though I shine.
    I touch dragons.
      I fly.

I tell myself – take flight!
Then you rise, chimera,
dark enough to swallow light.
I touch my power, shiver, doubt, recoil;
I take comfort in familiar toil.

It is the pain I know:
how to deal, how to play,
how to hide, how to stay…
I weigh power, I balance prey,
I gasp, I sigh—I silent pray…

And then, with all in balance,
all brinking at an end,
all shattered glass,
all rainbow blooded,

I jump, I fly, I dragonflooded,
my thoughts escape, my heart bursts,
beating…

    My wings are new, sticky, but completing.

Balance

DRAGONKEPT

the terror of loss
the fervent appeal
I know what I want
I know what I feel
there's a habit in holding
clutching tight, drawing deep
there's no reason pretending
grinding teeth while I sleep
I want it to be real
I want, beg and steal
but as soon as I drag
fingers through smoke
see clearly, see far
I see little hope
only wishes and wants
and pale imitation
nothing strong, little true
only sad limitations.

DRAGONFREED

I lie searching
frozen dreaming
hotblooded scheming
count mine the heartbeats
belonging to others and my longing.

I thirst – I would tear
throat out of love forsaken
die lonely, parched, unheeded
only wanting to be needed.

I will not fall in love.
I have been resident in that abyss
I have drunk and fed and laid abed
then woke alone,
unwed in heart and mind and body.

I will not fall in love again –
not fall but soar aloft –
crowd plane and hawk and eagle from the sky,
I will climb, explode and cry.

All will slide, slip and wildly cling
I will shudder, strengthen, fiercely sing
Then you might answer me….

DRAGONLOVED

I have loved you for years
I have feared you as well
I have done all and done nothing,
Done what I should.
Turned blind eye and soft heart and made up a story,
Desperately tried, failed and was sorry…
I wish you would stop, just listen to me -
I wish I knew how, when and what's true.
You were all that I wanted
I dreamed you and your skin
I reached and rejoiced
I refused to give in….
I wanted only truth from you
From me you wanted lies.

DRAGONBORNE

I am a dragon
I never sleep
Though my eyes may close

Dragon blood keeps me safe
Dragon bone dragon deep
Though my eyes may close

Not every thing's a story
Not every thing's a dream
Not everything bleeds
Not all is as it seems

When dragons cry
The heavens weep
What dragons wake
Is what they keep

I am the dragon in the room
Though my eyes may close
My breath not there
Never think I sleep

My skin is made of stories
My blood is made of dreams
And when I love
It is never what it seems.

# AFTER THE END

There is a Japanese art called "Kintsukuroi". It is a way of making something beautiful out of something broken. Shattered fragments are put back together with molten gold and silver. The piece is returned to its original shape but with all fractured lines held together by veins of precious metal. The scars are visible. The scars are what make each piece unique. And I think that is so for all of us. We all have scars from battle, win and lose, and the scars tell all our stories. We are held together by our healed wounds and we glitter like dragon treasure when the sun hits us.